Between Green and Orange

Thought Provoking Poems

To
Ini,
Enjoy!

Love.

Liz Mingo *Liz Mingo*

09/06/2023

xo

Who Am I?

I was born in the Commonwealth of Dominica, West Indies. I came to England in 1975, a very shy 10 year old! I started writing in the late 80's after being prompted by a friend. I didn't take my writing seriously until much later. As I got older, my poems were influenced by events that were happening in everyday life, being reported on the news and issues experienced by family and friends. I would describe my poetry as a bag of liquorice allsorts - you will laugh, cry, think, start a debate, maybe even relate!

From my head, to my fingers, to the page, to your mind, to your body, to your soul!

Thank You

To my Entire Family, whom I adore - words are not enough! You are My HEART!! Thank you ALL for the constant praise and encouragement.

To my Friends, whom I love – from my SiA crew, to my Magwells Posse, to my PJ Weekend Crew, to my PiK to ALL my friends – period!

A special Thank You to my friend Jumi, my Sister from another Mother. You started the juices flowing and have been reading me since day dot!

Contents

4PM

My favourite time of the day!
Monday to Monday
I know what's coming!
Our secret rendezvous
Just us two!
My friends say this should stop.
And I give it some thought.
But the closer it gets to 4PM
The quicker I ignore them!
They don't understand
About you and me
What we share is so special,
Wish we could start at 3!

8 4 6

In an ideal world
It should really only take 8 hours and 46 minutes
To convict -
The Police!

But we know the defence
Will want to build a fence
Around their client
Big him up as a hero; and
claim he's innocent!

They'll wanna paint George Floyd as the baddie.
But in all honesty
It won't be their fault, the law is an ass
And allows for such mockery!

They'll proceed to paint their picture.
When no space is left,
They'll rest!
The prosecution won't need a brush,
They have no canvas to wipe clean.
They simply need to run the recording.....

Derek Chauvin - kneeling
On George Floyd's neck!

Restricting his breathing,
Until he takes his final breath!
"I can't breathe".
Are the words he kept repeating.
Yet George Floyd was ignored and not respected as a
human being!

So, Derek Chauvin,
All eyes on YOU!
The world is watching
The clock is ticking - ***EIGHT***, 7, ***SIX***, 5, ***FOUR***....8 4 6....
No justice, no peace!

8:46!

Not talking about the next train out
Or the next flight to take off
I'm talking time on a clock.
Tick, Tock! Tick, Tock! Tick, Tock!....

Not talking about the time of day,
Although it could be read that way.
8 Minutes and 46 is specific!
Tick, Tock! Tick, Tock!, Tick!....

He's face down, on the ground.
Assumed the position!
They stand, in a nonchalant pose.
Chest pushed out, showing off to the world!
Tick, Tock! Tick, Tock!....

Knees locked!
Not an ounce of remorse
For the use of unnecessary force.
Their signature DNA!
So, it's just another day.
Tick, Tock, Tick!....

Even at almost 9 Minutes,
They didn't let George Floyd up.

He remained handcuffed!
For 8 Minutes and 46,
Time stood still!
Tick! Tock!....

He couldn't breathe, he said as much.
And after 8 Minutes and 46 seconds,
Clocks came to a permanent stop!
Tick, Tock! Tick, Tock! Tick, Tock! Tick, Tock!....
Sadly, another brother bites the dust.
Tick!....

A Love Letter (in Poetry Form)

Dear C-19,

How I wish that you end,
To enable me to spend
Time, precious time
In the arms of the one who once was mine!

12 months have passed since I last saw him
And sincerely, my patience is wearing thin!
I beg you put an end to this
So my lover and I may once again meet
To Hug, to kiss....
What bliss!
O how I wish....

When you have finally taken flight
My love and I can then unite
I plead then that you should go
With haste, and speed and by tomorrow!

Yours,
A Hopeless Romantic!

A Sonnet

May I?
But only if you will allow.
If the answer is Yes
May I caress
And trace
The outline of your face
You are like a flower, in bloom
Allow me the room
To sit a while, and admire
My heart desires....
I see thee, purely by touch
To many that is hardly enough
But me, I see your true beauty
Just with my hands!
The world is dark to me
But not you!
If I continue
To caress all night
By morning, my sight
Shall surely be restored!

Ask Me Again, Tomorrow

Don't mean to be a pain,
But can you say that again?
Sorry, I missed what you said.
Got too much going on in my head.
It's not you, it's me. I'm just so stressed!
But, ask me again, tomorrow and I'll probably say YES!

Asking for Help

Not sure where to start!
It's darn embarrassing, actually,
That something like this should come from me
I'm usually solid - a rock and then some!
But this time round, I must succumb....
To the fact that I'm drowning, and it's not pretty
I appreciate I've brought this on myself,
But, dear friend, I'm asking for help

Blue

It's not my favourite colour,
Cause it's how I feel sometimes
When you're not here
And I'm missing you!
But then I look up at the clear sky,
No clouds, just a bright blue
And my mind races to you
And that generates a smile.
And for a while,
I think my favourite colour could be BLUE!

By the Lake

We sit, legs crossed
Facing each other
You, my best friend, my lover.
The first time you said you loved me,
Our very first date,
ALL happened here, By the Lake!

Closing Arguments!

Just seen this headline,
Bold as can be!
Doesn't need spelling out.
It's clearly about George Floyd!

I should have faith,
But I'm shaking, in all honesty.
What if Derek Chauvin is found not guilty!

Wanna be positive
And believe he will be
But we're talking [dis]United States
Corrupt systems, Corrupt Cops
That's how America operates!

Justice is truly deserved!
And Derek Chauvin needs to serve
Time
For the heinous crime
He's committed!

Closing Arguments....

I'm gonna **believe!**

Covid-19!

I'm angry with Covid-19,
The way it happened, no warning!
Took everyone by surprise, not just me
So not sure I could have done anything differently
In all honesty.

It is what it is, but an absolute pain!
I've so missed the Theatre
Not sure I'll ever go again.
Just wouldn't feel comfy
Having that many people around me.

Probably a tad pedantic
And over the top with panic
Totally caused by this pandemic!
Usually I'd be the first to say YES,
But, wouldn't feel ready, even with a covid test!

Meeting up with friends was such a blast.
But now, sadly, a thing of the past.
Piccadilly Circus, Leicester Square, Chinatown.
Our ladies nights out were so much fun!

Covid-19!
Some days bad, some good.

Plays havoc with one's mood
Which is clearly not good....
For our mental health!
But the onus is on us,
To remain positive and focused.

I must admit,
I'm kinda liking online shopping
No fuss, no queuing - wot bliss!
But, what I really do miss,
Is not being able to socialise.
Although, the flip side of that - My bank balance is
permanently in the black!

I hear there are rumours of a 4th lockdown
Bring it on, I say!
I'm certainly prepared for what comes next
Lesson learned -
The pantry is stacked high with Andrex!

Depression

What does depression look like?
Is it wanting to be alone,
Cutting off oneself from the outside world.
Is it wanting to be in a dark place,
With covers pulled up so high it covers your face?
No communication.
'Nil by mouth' like before and after an operation.

Is depression even a look?
It's certainly not partial,
It's on speed dial.
Can consume in a flash,
Like a scabby rash!
Sweeps aside colour, religion, race
Depression does not discriminate!

Is depression a feeling?
A state of mind
From deep within.
Self-inflicting?
Perhaps not initially but left untreated will take over your
every being
And resign yet another, to mental suffering!

Depression is negative vibes,
And will take over your life; if you let it!
Negativity breeds negativity
Creates Despondency
Eats away at your confidence
Layer after layer after layer
Until there's nothing left, and you stand naked -
Transparency!

With confidence stripped, you hit rock bottom!
There are offers of help, but you decline them.
Instead, insisting on putting on a brave face.
For whom? And why?
Depression should not be ignored.
This shit is real; no longer taboo.
Makes no sense to hide behind it.
Admission is key, to getting back on your feet!

Give Depression a face – be seen
Give Depression a voice – be heard.
Stand tall; educate the world.
Don't suffer in silence, give Depression a platform!

Distinction

(a difference or contrast between similar things)

Gun - lethal, used to propel bullets.
Taser - non-lethal, used to incapacitate.
They also differ in size and weight
Yet, a police officer, with over 20 years' experience couldn't
differentiate.
Or were her actions deliberate?

She needed to deploy more thinking time
You know, maybe 8minutes 46 or even 9minutes 29!
Before making up her mind
to pull from her dominant side
'Cause then, a young, black kid would still be alive!

"Holy shit I just shot him" was all she had to say
After killing Daunte.
A coincidence? A mistake?
In the wake
Of the Derek Chauvin trial,
For murdering George Floyd.
Either way, the damage was done
A mother prepares to bury her son!

Hindsight, O, hindsight....
Where were you,
When said Officer, Kimberly Potter,
Reached for her *Revolver*
Instead of her *Taser*!

She failed to make the DISTINCTION
Her actions....
Further propelling the black race into *Extinction*
BUT, don't believe their hype.
WE here for the DURATION!

The above is just my opinion
And some may say it's wrong, but
Let's check the facts....
DEAD - young kid - BLACK
SHOOTER - Police Officer - WHITE
Not saying I'm right
Just that....
Something isn't **WRIGHT**!

Face-Off (with a Cat)

Stood in the kitchen
Eating a tuna sarnie
Saw a reflection in the glass and realised it was me.
Not liking this lockdown body!

Looked out onto the garden
Another day, same difference
Except for a cat, perched on the neighbour's fence
It had a big belly!
Not unlike mine, actually.
Hmmmm, pot calling the kettle...
My audacity!

Kitty was probably thinking the same
It stayed there a while,
Knowingly invading my space.
We locked eyes!
Did it want a face - off?
Or some of my tuna sarnie?
Maybe said cat was hungry!

So, out of respect for this possibly hungry cat, which
wasn't mine,
I ceased chewing. I stared back
Primed, and ready for combat!

"Listen here feline
You're not mine
So be gone, make tracks!
Remove your brown & black
fur from my vision
Before I perform an execution!"

Meow....

"Bugger off. On your way,
Go find your home, your owners...
Or are you a stray?
So long, farewell, Auf Wiedersehen...."....
I must be freaking insane!
Am I gonna let a cat get the better of me?
Invade my privacy, disrupt my daily routine - not
happening!
So, I did the next best thing and showed it who was boss -
Grabbed the rest of my sarnie and ran upstairs!

Friday Hype!

I swear, Friday hype
Is totally psychological!
Just knowing
I can vegetate for the next 2 days doing anything or
nothing!
Whatever that looks like,
I'll always be ready to write
Never too far from pen & pad!
It's my prerogative
To always be ready
Never happier than when I'm writing Poetry!

Grenfell

If you don't know about this tragedy
Where have you been?
I can recall exactly where I was, and what I was doing.
Can never forget June 2017!

I'm sure like me, focus was for those trapped inside
Clearly now frantic
In a panic
About how to get out - alive!
But without being involved first-hand,
One could neither relate nor understand!

But there were those who were,
and who can.
They were up close, and personal.
In the thick of it - literally!
The Fire Service First Responders showed courage and
bravery!
No time to think, no time to feel
Numb to the soul
Emotions on hold
Whilst battling a raging fire!

Grenfell was almost 4 years ago, yet it's still very raw!
Innocent lives were lost

For the sake of cutting costs!
Grenfell Tower housed human beings.
Over 70 of whom lost their lives, on that fateful night
But for the Firefighters, it would have been more!

They may not have died physically,
But mentally,
They are scarred for life!
Mental health issues and PTSD
are their legacy!

Inspired by RN. A Grenfell Firefighter

Guilty!

Even after a guilty verdict
There are still some who won't accept it!
Counts 1, 2 & 3 - Guilty as hell!
And that's where he should be.
Derek Chauvin isn't a hero, he's a bully!
And all White Supremacists
Need to own it!

The world is truly twisted
When a racist Kkkop is still being
supported!
A Felon! A Convict!
No regard for the badge
Nor for human life!
Didn't give George Floyd a chance.
No respect for his pledge of allegiance,
Nor to protect and serve.
Now he's got exactly what he deserves!

Guilty, x 3
Job done!
Now he's locked up, throw away the key.
Justice has been reached - finally!
First and foremost for George's Family,
And then for EVERYBODY!

Not just the black Community.
Said Justice needs to bring about harmony!

This outcome offers a glimmer of hope.
It may be tiny, but it's there,
And it starts with the aptly named
George Floyd Square.
One can visit, sit, reminisce
And know that George Floyd is at peace!

The world would rather George Floyd was here,
But this Brother hasn't died in vain!
The world will forever feel his pain,
And always remember his name!

Harris & Pence (US Debate)

O yeah, I stayed up for this!
2am UK time but I didn't care.
It was worth staying up
To witness the fly land on Mike Pence's hair!
Maybe he's got 'shit' for brains!

It didn't just fly on and fly off
It made sure to stay a while.
Made itself very comfy
His forehead sure was sweaty!

No-one watching could miss it -
The sweat, the fly or the hand
Which he got when trying to butt in....
"Mr Vice President, I'm SPEAKING!"
"I'm SPEAKING!"
Let's hope Joe Biden was watching!

This is how you do it!!

Even seated, she stood tall.
Held her own!
Demanded her time back from 'Susan' Page
When Mr Pence stole seconds of hers
Which put her in a slight rage.

She oozed power.
Knowledge personified!
He in turn, sat there, slowly developing a red eye!

Was it the pressure of the night?
Fatigue, or maybe conjunctivitis.
Truth be told, they're Politicians
So, could have just been Poli-Tricks!

Don't get me wrong,
Now that the debate is done
Neither have changed my beliefs
About politicians or politics!
However, she is WOMAN, just like me
And she showed the world how to deal with a bully!

Power, Woman, Black
Black, Woman, Power
Write it in whatever order!
Mike Pence & Kamala Harris...
Yes, I lost sleep, but this debate was Lit!

Hero

The Matriarch,
A Queen
My protector!
From birth, and still
In me you instilled
Nothing but goodness,
Self-love and forgiveness!
My Dearest
Grandma,
You're the greatest!
I love you so
You're my undisputed *Hero*....
Yesterday, today, tomorrow!

Hoodies!

On street corners you see them, loitering with intent
A menace to society and seemingly hell bent
On portraying unhealthy behaviour
But is it meant?
Or simply an act to impress!

On street corners you see them, dappled in shades of grey
Hiding their identity, the hooded way!
Gangly legs and spotty ashen faces
They are most at home in dark and rancid places!

On buses and trains, you see them, with feet on seats
Carrying on like they darn well own it!
Lacking in manners as they hail abuse and profanity.
But again, is it meant?
Or an act to impress society?

Heartless
Obscene
Obnoxious
Dunce
Ignorant
Embarrassing
Stupid

H O O D I E S!

I Am....

Think you know me?
I'm more than what you see
Standing before you
I'm extraordinary!

See me on the football pitch
I dazzle
Left-foot, Right-foot, switch
Quick as lightening
Can't catch me
Got mad skills.
The name's LIZ though
Not Hope Solo!

See me on the badminton court
Quick flick of the wrist
and serve be on you!
Backhand, forehand, drop shot, smash!
Drop shot, forehand, backhand,
Smash!
In your face - Rematch?
Bring it!
No fear.
'Cause my racquets be Yonex!

See me with pen and pad
London's greatest bard!
Give me a topic
Watch me drop an Acrostic
Or maybe a Sonnet - "Shall I...."
Damn, William's already done it!
So maybe I'll just freestyle.
Take it slow,
And let the juices flow.

See me
I am....
Extraordinary!

Ice Cubes in Glasses

I know people may hate this
And no, it's not a fetish!
But, for some unknown reason,
Just Love the clink clink of ice cubes in glasses!
Can't say when this started really
But why I love this sound is beyond me!

If You Love Me

We need to talk....
I appreciate that sounds ominous,
And it is. It's about US!
The aim isn't to hurt you,
But I need to be true!
-can't do this anymore.
I'm so sorry. I truly am.
Breakups are never easy, but,
If you love me....
You'll understand?

It's Ok!

Yesterday you were fine
Today the stars don't align
There's nothing wrong with you
So, quit beating yourself up
And don't allow your head to drop.
It's ok!

Shit happens on a daily
Even when we least expect
Don't be crying over spilt milk,
'Cause it's already on the floor!
Simply pour yourself some more.
It's ok!

No two days are the same
Some are good, some bad
The rest are sent to try us
It's imperative to not lose focus.
Keep on, keeping on!
Better days will come.
So, don't feel no way,
It's ok!

We were not built of bricks
So, admitting defeat
Does not render you weak!
Help is there if you need it.
Life is a constant struggle

When you're living in a concrete jungle!
So, scream, shout
Reach out.
It's ok!

Today may be my time to shine,
Tomorrow, yours!
We're all on a merry-go-round called life.
We journey through revolving doors
And none of us are exempt.
Not the rich, not the poor!
So, don't suffer in silence,
Buckle up, show resilience!
It'll be ok!

Heartbreak is not defined by status.
So, don't shy away
Tomorrow is another day
A new chapter begins.
Embrace the mistakes!
Put your best foot forward - ready, set, go
Don't allow others to dictate your pace,
This is your race!
And that's ok! It's ALL ok!

It Wasn't....

It wasn't about the way she delivered that poem,
at the Inauguration.
Or even about the respect
she showed to President Biden and the other guests.

It wasn't about the way she held herself,
the confidence which oozed from her whilst on stage,
Even at her young age!

It wasn't that she shared said stage with a President, a
Doctor,
a Vice President; and an Attorney.
For me,
Amanda Gorman stole the show!
A young sister
Who only a few years ago,
Had difficulty saying the letter "R"
Because of a speech impediment.
It certainly didn't disrupt her flow!

It wasn't even that the Poem was Amazing
"The Hill We Climb" embracing
So much positivity and truth!
All that aside, the highlight for me,
As she stood there, with that glow,
Was her coat, in my favourite colour - Yellow!

It Was Raining...

Planned to go for a walk
But,
It was raining.
So now I'm wondering....
Do I still go?
Stick to my plans and brave it
Or retreat and admit defeat!
Giving up is not in my DNA,
So on went the wellies and the mac......
I may have a fab story to share when I get back!

Jealous?

I'm black and I'm proud!
I stand tall!
Walk with a swagger.
Talk with authority.
Are you jealous of me?

I'm proud to be black!
I am power!
My strength appears to rile you,
Hence the constant profanity.
Are you jealous of me?

I'm black and I'm proud!
I'm sassy!
You try your best to emulate,
Continually....
The clothes I wear, the moves I make.
Are you jealous of me?

I'm proud to be black!
I continue to shine!
Is that the reason for your anger?
Why you insist on using N.I.G.G.E.R
Even now, in the 21st century!
Are you jealous of me?

I'm black and I'm proud!
It's my trait!
You being You isn't my responsibility.
I'm BLACK, originally!!!!
Is that why you're jealous of me?

I'm black and I'm proud!
Never need a fake tan.
I wear a permanent gloss!
A-ha! Finally, the penny drops!
That's why you're jealous of US!

So You....

Hail abuse.
Disrespect.
Your knees connect,
With our necks!
On a regular,
To the jugular!
A Brother cries out in pain; and
The knees tighten on the veins!

Yes, I'm black and I'm proud!
I am unique!
As are you?
Remove the blinkers and find your place....
Alongside me, WE are the human race!!

Let's Talk!

Let's talk about it
Mental health
It's not about colour, it's not about wealth
So, let's talk about it!
Can attack, real quick – like a bullet
Or gradually,
When we least expect it!
But the effects are the same – negative vibes on the brain!
Let's not waste another second
Losing sight of what's important
Can we please just talk about it!

Let's Talk about Race

Let's talk about race
Let's talk about you and me
Let's talk inclusion and equality
And all that we can do for society!

Let's talk race instead of diversity
Last time I checked it was the 21st century!
I am here, therefore I belong
So extend your olive branch and make me feel welcome!

What do you see when you look at me?
A face which doesn't conform to type?
So you entertain the hype!
And my name, what does it tell you?
"It's unpronounceable so she'll add no value!"

You see colour, I see ME
Intelligent, strong, organically hyped
You assume I'm ready for a fight
But no fists here, so lose the racial stereotype!

Let's talk race, instead of diversity
Allow me the room to tell my story
Hear what I've got to say.
Listen to my voice, not pointless surveys!

Let's talk race, instead of diversity
Find out what makes me tick
My beliefs
What makes me, ME!
And before you blindly discriminate,
Let my actions dictate
My ability!

Let's talk race,
Let's talk equality
Let's talk inclusivity
In fact....
Let's just talk!

Life

I wake from sleep,
Yet another day to greet,
To drink, to eat
To speak....
With Friends and Family!
No two days are the same,
This is true.
Challenges to face,
Some good, some bad!
Some moments happy, others sad.
But whilst I breathe and have life in me,
I'll spend the days writing Poetry!

Loss!

We agreed to commit,
So I don't get it!
Why the sudden change of heart?
You swore you loved me!
But, suddenly,
We're drifting apart.
What's got you acting this way?
I'm at a loss to understand,
Why you've chosen to walk away!

Love Me, or Leave Me

Are we ever gonna be the real deal?
You treat me like shit
And I'm tired of it!
Can we have a conversation?
This situation - isn't healthy!
Can't take it anymore.
So unless you're sure...
Love Me, or Leave Me!
Which one will it be?
Actually,
On second thoughts,
I'm calling the shots - get lost!

Mirror

Mirror mirror on the wall
Who is the fairest of them all?
Dear mirror, that was rhetorical!
I am the fairest, the queen bee
I don't need a nursery rhyme
To define me!
I look into you, not through
And what shines back,
Is a reflection of beauty - black!
Dear mirror,
Whilst you may have pride of place,
By hanging tall or rested on a surface,
Let's not get this twisted!
Know your place, and let's be true -
You don't use me, I use YOU!

Morning Affirmation

I'm alive!
Hip hip hip hooray....
Another day
to....
Start my love affair,
With Prayer!
Not forgetting to own my space,
And put a smile on someone else's face

Morning Affirmation

Wake from sleep
Yet another day to greet
Use it
- wisely!
Others were not so lucky
- sadly!
Another chance
- Pray and give Thanks!

Morning Affirmation

Goooood morning!
Rise and be ready to shine.
Yes YOU!
Why not YOU!
The Lord saw fit to grant...
Another day
So don't entertain *CAN'T*!
Own the highway
Strut down that runway....
With purpose. Own it!
Rise and be ready to shine!

Negligence

I sit
I stare....
Into space
So much to do,
Yet I procrastinate!
Can anyone else relate?
This isn't me!
What utter negligence
From my lack of diligence!
I need to motivate myself,
Cause this isn't good for my mental health!

News

Ok, so got the memo
Not sure I even wanted to know.
Guess they had to tell me
'Cause it's about family.
But no remorse here - sorry!

Didn't need this piece of news
Why even send it
To get my views?
Don't feel no way!
Got nothing to say!
So let me be
'Cause I'm at peace now - finally!

Delete!

Maybe the next memo -
All items 50% off @ Costco....
Now that's the kinda news I want to know!

No Joy

In the case of Joy Gardner versus the Police,
They were all found 'not guilty' and the case dismissed.
Even before the trial began, the outcome was clear.
The case between the Police and Joy Gardner was totally
unfair!

Is there no justice in this world, not even for the dead?
"She was a beast who needed taming" is what the Police
said.
Joy Gardner was a human being, she wasn't a criminal.
Yet the Police gagged and bound her like she was an
animal!

Joy Gardner should have been no more than a deportee
And the Police could have handled the situation
differently.
Instead, they used 13 feet of tape around her neck like
they were handling a slave
And due to their actions, Joy Gardner is no more, she lies
dead in a grave!

In the case of Joy Gardner versus the Police,
There was No Joy in the verdict and there is yet to be
justice!

"Beast", "Raging Bull", "Crocodile" are words the Police used to describe Joy Gardner.
And in their years of service they had never come across anyone like her.
In a 12-year reign as Police Officers in the Police Force, They had never encountered murderers or rapists who were more dangerous?

In the case of Joy Gardner versus the Police, They had a chance to tell their story, they were able to say their piece.
But Joy Gardner is gone from this world and she won't be back.
She has no chance to tell her story – the Police made sure of that!

The Jury said "acquit", not "convict" and the Police roam free
They have their lives, whilst Joy Gardner lies in the cemetery!
The Police said they used "reasonable force" and their actions were "justified".
How can that be when the injuries Joy Gardner sustained is the reason she died!

Offside!

I'm a female, with a football
At my feet.
Get over it!
I'm a female and I play.
And guess what, I'm not gay.

So enough with that stereotype,
Don't believe the hype!

I'm a female, with a football.
Got mad skills
Like Marta,
Sam Kerr, and Rapinoe
And best keeper ever is Hope Solo!

I'm a female who loves football.
I can talk Messi, Marcelo, Manè
Salah, Suàrez, Sanè
Perisic, Modric or Mandzukic.
Take your pick!

Can you talk Miedema, Alex Morgan, Marozsán,
Le Sommer, Gill Scott, Wang Shuang,
Nikita Parris, Christen Press or Patrizia Panico,
Didn't think so!

I'm a female baller and I got game!
Can do more keep ups than Pogba,
Score more headers than Drogba!
So when you see me on the pitch,
Support and respect; or bring it!

I can *Cruyff* you in my sleep!

Women's football has arrived,
And is on the rise.
Hopefully it's here to stay,
So Y.N.W.A!
But way too soon to tackle equal pay!

From Aguero's last minute winner
against QPR
To Liverpool's miracle comeback in Istanbul
Women love football too; and yes
We *do* understand the offside rule!

Paradise

To be with you
On any given day,
Of any given month,
In any given year...
To have you wipe away the tears
Which moist my cheeks.
To land a passionate kiss
On your sweeter than sweet lips.
To have all these moments,
And much more besides.
That is paradise in my eyes!

Player, Player!

In a bar, in a club
I clock him
Eyes locked, contact made
Names and numbers exchanged!
No longer want him to be a stranger; so
Idle chit-chat, kick-start a convo
Need to know
If we're speaking the same lingo!

We hit the dance floor - Foxtrot, Tango
Salsa, Rumba, Slow jams
His hands....
All over!
I move in closer; ready to devour....
This catch; my main course!
Ay papi! Make we wanna speak Spanish!
But first, need to establish....

His status, and whether there's a future for us.
Moving a little fast I know, but
He had me at "hello!".
Yes, an old, familiar cliché
But hey,
He just had me – period!

The weeks fly by

And the question is 'when' not 'if'

I'm gonna get up close and personal with this guy

This may be premature, but I wanna be the MRS to his MR!

So, I hang on to his every word

Believe him when he tells me

That we'll be together – eventually!

For now, I should be patient and not worry.

But what I begin to understand

As contact becomes less and less frequent

Is that this guy doesn't do commitment!

He's a Player and the Player just played me!

Practice

Ok, so I've tried and tried
But I keep failing!
I'm just not getting it.
It's way too hard
And I'm tired!
But I shouldn't give up
To be honest
I need to keep going!
The only way I'll get the hang of this
Is to Practice! Practice! Practice!

Rise!

The road may have been rough,
You may have had it tough
The same can be said for many of us
Everyone has a story.
Some are innocent and sweet,
Others harbour lies and deceit!

Your innocence may have been taken
Your childhood stolen
By the very person
Who should have been your protector
Instead, you inherited a monster!

Your life becomes a living hell.
You suffer in silence, too frightened to tell.
But you show resilience! Find an inner strength!
To RISE up, and, SPEAK up.
YOU ARE Beauty,
Said monster is the beast!

Let your innocence shine through, from your head to your toes
Hide no more, the world needs to know!
So, Rise Up, Speak Up!
Shout it from the rooftops!

Perpetuate hope, so that....
You, Me, Us
Can ALL Rise Up;
And make our voices heard!

Safety

Before I met you,
I was drowning....
In my own self-pity!
But you rescued me.
Pulled me to safety, and
Out of harm's way!
My Dearest Knight....
In armour - you shine.
The future is bright, because
I am now yours and you are now mine!

Seeing Red!

I'm five days late
Should I start to celebrate?
I rush to the loo
With my Clear Blue!

The anticipation is killing me
So, I look away, albeit reluctantly!
Will blue be my favour colour when this test is done
Or will I need to stock up on more tampons?

I'm five days late
Should I start to celebrate?
My head is already at Mothercare
Checking out clothes and a Maclaren pushchair!

I'm so excited, should I tell someone?
My hubby first, then I'll call my mum
But maybe not wise to get anyone else involved
Until I know the outcome of the test result!

I'm five days late, almost a week
That's got to mean something – hasn't it?
I'm five days late, I'm five days late
But hold on, did I even ovulate?

I'm five days late in coming on
In nine months' time I could be a mum!
I've had all the symptoms –
Light-headedness, eating for two,
Nausea and frequent visits to the loo!

Ok, so I've sat here for long enough,
Wondering whether I'm pregnant or not.
Time to check the stick –
But hold on, what's this?
I'm seeing RED – goddammit!

Street Crime

We continue to fight this pandemic
I'm not talking Covid,
I'm talking guns, loaded!
And knives....
Taking young lives!

Black on Black crime
Back on the rise.
Youngers, get wise
You're killing your own kind!
Lose the arrogance, this isn't a joke,
Wise up, and, stay woke!

Strength

Life can be tough!
Even when I'm feeling rough,
The aim is to keep going!
Find a way to shine
By showing....
I can cope,
By not giving up hope!
It's not easy,
But it's up to me,
So, I keep the faith!
And though all seems lost
I'm finding the strength to put my trust -
In God!

Sus....

You felt the need to stop me
Now you're asking questions, accusingly.
You say I look suspicious
I ask if it's the colour of my skin.
You say it's not a race thing.
I apologise for stating, the obvious!
You felt the need to stop me
Now you look on with contempt.
Your demeanour says *guilty*, until proven innocent!
You felt the need to stop me
Yet your reasons hold no weight
So I stand here, perplexed.
"What's next, Mr Officer, Your Knee, my Neck?"

Tales

I have so many tales to tell....
Where to begin?
Stories of old or stories of new
Stories about me or stories about you?
Or perhaps tales of us two....
About how we met, and fell in love - will those do?

The Affair

Five minutes here,
Five minutes there
In fact, any second, they have to spare
In order to see each other and continue this affair!

This is but a liaison, and a dangerous one at that
For which love itself does not really play a part
It is selfishness, and a hunger for lust
The danger, the excitement, the adrenalin rush!

She will not leave her husband, he will not leave his wife
So, why prolong this affair and ruin other people's lives?
What then when all hell breaks loose, and the shit hits the fan?
Which it will. So broken hearts are a foregone conclusion!

This affair has become a compulsive obsession!
With stolen moments of heart pumping passion.
But innocent children suffer with the upkeep of this secret
So, at the end of the day is this affair truly worth it?

Ten minutes here,
Ten minutes there.
In fact, any minute they have to spare
Which allows them to carry on with this affair!

He can't stop, she can't stop
They can't stop!
But someone needs to,
Otherwise this affair will destroy more than just two
people!

The Black Man

A towering inferno -
Virile, solid and strong
Like a piece of rump steak that's extremely well done!

The Black Man - Denzel Washington, Rodney King,
Malcolm X, Spike Lee
And of course the one who fathered me!

Undoubtedly second to none -
Incomparable, and in a word unique.
From the hairstyle on his head to his fine physique.
In a class by himself and a sight for sore eyes,
From his glittering white teeth, to the weapon behind his
flies!

The Black Man - Nelson Mandela, Mohammed Ali,
Sidney Poitier and that African brother, Kunta Kinte!

With hands as tough as steel, yet soft enough to caress
And a dress sense all his own, that leave others on the
doorstep.

The Black Man - Steve Biko, Edward Earl Johnson,
Hector Pieterson, Bob Marley, Martin Luther King, the
brother who had a dream!

The Black Man - truly one in a million, truly a work of art.
Like a painting by Picasso,
or a masterpiece by Mozart!

The Black Woman

A pillar of strength standing tall and bold
With as pure a completion as 24 carat gold!
In a class by herself, and a force to be reckoned with
God's greatest creation - that is my belief!

The Black Woman - Mariam Makeba, Rosa Parks, Harriet
Tubman, Oprah Winfrey, Kamala Harris - the list, is
endless!

With beauty beyond compare from her head to her toes
The ingredients for which imitators long to know
No amount of sun or lotion can create this effect see
Cause the Nubian Sister is one in a million - an
originality!

The Black Woman - Maya Angelou, Alice Walker,
Coretta Scott King, Betty Shabbaz, and the one who gave
birth to me - to whom I say "thanks and RIP!"

The Black Woman - of which only a select few can be.
I am a select few and The Black Woman is me!

The Breakup

Sit,
Let's talk
Unless you wanna walk?
Either is cool with me,
Wanna make sure you're comfortable!

Don't take this the wrong way
I do still care about you
It's just that, these things you do
You know, with the cat poo
And having the dog lick you
They're too much, way too much,
I've simply had enough!

This is real tough,
But you get the reason for the breakup - right?
I could deal with the OCD,
And you always cleaning up after me
Even popping your pimples just before a meal
Wasn't too much of a big deal
I was cool with that,
But that thing with the cat....

I love pussy too,
But I could never get used to that!

The Little Things!

O what bliss.
I'd forgotten how at peace
One can be
Whilst having a soak in the bath!
It's usually showers for me,
But this was welcomed respite from a day which began
way too early!
Such tranquillity, and inspiration too....
My next piece may come whilst I'm sat on the loo.
Note to self - always have pen & paper at the ready!

The Other Woman

What does she have that I'm lacking,
Which makes life with her that more interesting?
What takes you back to her every once in a while,
Is it that she has a more radiant smile?

What does she do that I no longer can?
Which now makes her your No.1 fan?
I thought I'd be your No.1 for life
When I said, "I do" and agreed to be your wife!

What have I done suddenly that's made you stray?
And has you coming home smelling of her body spray!
What's the reason for this sudden change – something I
did or said
Or is it that you find her more adventurous in bed?

I too could be adventurous, just give me the chance to
show
That like her I can do things which would give you that
certain glow!
After all, I too am woman made up of sugar and spice
So, what is it about her that makes her extra nice?

There's nothing she possesses which cannot be found in
me.

I have the face, the breasts, the vagina, and the to die for
body!
But you've had your cake and eaten it and I'm willing to
let this slide.
Yet am at a loss to understand your need for this liaison
on the side!

Ok, so humans we all are and capable of doing wrong
And who she was isn't important, but what is, is that we
now move on
I'm ready and willing to do this if you feel the same
But there will be no repeat performance of this situation
again – right?

Too Young To Die

Dead, dead, dead and gone
Killed by a knife or was it a gun?
He shouldn't have died, his death was a mistake.
His life taken away by those who practice hate!

Dead, dead, dead and gone
No longer here to have any fun.
A young, innocent brother with his whole life ahead.
Ended by racist bigots with no brain in their head!

Dead, dead, dead and gone
He was somebody's child, he was somebody's son.
A senseless killing, and how many more like this
Before people of all races learn to live in peace!

Dead, dead, dead and gone
Taken too soon, taken too young
What grief for his family, what tears they must cry.
STEPHEN LAWRENCE was too Young to Die!

Trump & Biden (US Debate)

Can't believe I stayed up for this!
2am UK time. I elected to lose sleep
So I could watch these 2 heavyweights, Trump & Joe
Go toe to toe!
Instead, they were more like clowns
Fighting it out in a playground!

Trump & Biden, aka Donald & Daffy
Both with a great opportunity
To endear themselves to the American people
Instead, it was an immature fist fight
What a load of tripe!

Even Mr Wallace, or is that Wally,
Who played Devil's Advocate, came across as weak
No balls! and slightly in fear of the Muppet?
Biden came across as placid and quite sweet
But I think he missed a trick!
Should have showed more gumption
And demanded the Republican shut up
Not make it a polite question!

He may have gained more respect
And probably more votes too
From Obama lovers and the BAME community

Especially with Trump-et unwilling to denounce white supremacy!

Anyway, it was what it was
In the very early hours!
I must admit,
At some point I did fall asleep!
Should have remained in my slumber
But I woke again, and listened a little more....
Did I miss anything of any significance?

Yawn yawn.

I pledge allegiance....
To no longer lose sleep by being a participating audience!

Wedded Bliss?

"With this ring I thee wed...."
How proud I was saying those words
Wanting nothing more than to be your wife
And to look forward to a wonderful married life

Yet, no sooner was the honeymoon over
You flipped the script and made me begin to wonder
And as your fist unexpectedly met my jaw,
I realised what I'd agreed to let myself in for!

The sheer shock of your actions alleviated the pain
But was this a one-off or would it happen again!
Who was this monster who now stood before me?
Treating me with contempt instead of lovingly!

What happened to the promises to treat me right?
And to whisper sweet nothings in my ear as you held me
tight.
What of the promises to keep me safe, and to cherish?
Where was the man I fell in love with?

Where was the tenderness you once displayed?
The ability to make me laugh, the romantic days

The passion, the zest for life and that sweet, sweet smile
Clearly all an act, 'cause now you're just hostile!

If I knew back then, what I know now.
I would never have committed to wedding vows!

What!

2018 and still I write about this
2018 and guns and knives continue to rule the streets!
Gun shots, stabbings....
2018 and still we got black on black killings
Today's youth need educating!

Postcode ain't right - gunshot
Live on the wrong side - gunshot
What's it gonna take to get these teens on the straight and
narrow
So they can live beyond tomorrow!

But today's youth should already know!
They should already know wrong from right
So, what are their reasons for continuing the street fight?
Is it simply that they can't see eye to eye, or, does it go
deeper still?
A need for recognition, affiliation....
To a gang, a crew, a need to belong, to fit in.....
somewhere, anywhere and by any means!

Is it a cry for help, a craving for a gap to be filled?
an empty void called LOVE!

Granted, the path to life is not always straight
There are trials and tribulations along the way,
and hurdles at every bend
But today's youth need to understand their route only lead
to dead endz!

What's it gonna take to make things ok
Whatever it's gonna take needs to start today!

What I Love About ME

I love that I am ME!
And I say that with authority.
I am unique, of course
As are all of us, but...
Even if I were a twin
I'd still be ME, with my authenticity!
I love that I can engage those unknown to me
Purely by my poetry!

What Went Wrong?

What went wrong between us – tell me?
Make me understand, make me see.
When we were together, I was so happy.
So, what went wrong between you and me?

What went wrong with you and I?
I thought I'd found my ideal guy
You wanted me and I wanted you
So what went wrong between us two?

What went wrong that you're no longer mine
I thought we'd be together till the end of time.
Something went wrong and I'd like to know
What went wrong that you had to go?

You were everything to me,
I really loved you!
So what went wrong if you loved me too?

Was it that you were like chalk and I was like cheese
Or that you liked your rice plain
And I liked mine with peas?
Was it that you said chips when I said fries,
Or was it that we just didn't compromise?

What went wrong?

Who is He?

Head down in the trash
Searching for scraps!
Leftovers from the night before
Whilst the queue from Pret spills out the door!

The first bin offers up nothing to his satisfaction
He moves away, his face a picture of resignation.
He hurries along, trying to find another,
Where are his family – his father, his mother?

From where has he come to end up like this?
Homeless, alone and on the streets?
Surely not a life one would willingly choose,
So perhaps abandoned from birth or even abused.

Who is he?
What is his name?

But is his name of any relevance?
And is who he is of any real importance!
What is certain is that he is human, like me
It is circumstance which has been unkindly!

Head down in the trash
Desperately searching for scraps….

Why?

Why couldn't he talk to me?
Let me know what was going on.
That he could no longer cope
Is it because he was a bloke?

Why could he not express
That his life had become a mess
Or that he was in way over his head.
Something, anything, instead he's dead!

Took his own life. Ended it. Just like that!
Now what?
Got all these f-ing questions!
Not a hint! Not a clue!
His legacy is a jigsaw puzzle.

"Selfish!"
Is that fair,
Or does it mean I don't care?
I'm still very angry, and in shock!
Yet here I am, trying to connect the dots.
Piece, after piece, after piece.
How the hell do I live with this?

We were best mates
Yet he couldn't open up.
What the FCUK!
I failed him big time.
Should have seen the signs!
I know he wouldn't blame me,
He'd want me to move on.
But that's easier said than done!

If he called now, I'd drop everything and run......
But he won't. He's gone!

RIP my friend!

Will You?

If I ask, will you be honest?
I'm not looking to pick a fight
But what I'd really like
Is for you to come clean, and spill the beans!

Loving you was a mistake,
I know that now.
Never should have exchanged vows!
But, c'est la vie,
It's on me!
But for once, just man up....
Did you FCUK - my best friend?

Without saying I Love You

My love,
Give me your hand
Let me caress it with mine
Let me hold it a while
Until it generates a smile
On that beautiful face!
Here, right now, in this place
We are one.
We share an embrace,
Whilst side by side in bed.
Silence is golden!
We need but a gaze,
The obvious need not be said!

Wondering

Been wondering how others are coping
You know, how they're getting on, with the current
situation
It's unprecedented times for all of us that's true,
But the old adage of "there's always someone worse off
than you" occupies my thoughts
Wish it did not
But, guess I'm that person.

Been wondering about those with not enough to eat
Those living rough, sleeping on the streets.
The vulnerable!
Those being abused!
Probably more now than ever.
When is the world going to weather, this storm.
This pandemic is claiming lives
In more ways than one!

Been wondering, if anyone else has been wondering, like
me.
Perhaps it's all unnecessary anxiety; but,
Just been wondering....

You

I love you!
I love you so much I swear it's a sin
I try and fight it
But it's a fight I'm not winning!

I love you!
I love you so much it's painful
I'm way too gone for medication
Like drugs, you're an addiction!

I love you!
I love you so much I'm blinkered!
Not only unable to find my way,
But also, in terms of what I want to say!

I love you!
I love you so much I can't think straight!
Thoughts of you engulf my entire being
And then of course, I'm unable to concentrate!

I love you!
I love you so much a day without you is unbearable
So undoubtedly, if it were possible,
I'd want to be with you 24/7!

I love you!
But if the message is still not clear
From what you've read here,
I cannot elaborate much more than to repeat,
I love you! I love you! I love you! – got it!

You Make Me....

You make me shiver
You make me…..
Forget what it is I wanted to say.
Why do you affect me in this way?

You make me wanna….
Burst out in song and never stop
You make me unafraid to try something new
What is it about you?

You make me tight-lipped and unable to speak,
And as for the rest of me – uncontrollably weak.
You make me wanna call you a thousand times a day,
And yet with nothing logical or sensible to say!

You make me wanna hold you and never let go
And whisper in your ear things which would be illegal for
sure!
Each mention of your name meets my face with a smile
And every thought of you puts me on a high!

You make me so nervous I break out in a sweat
And it's been this way from the first time we met!
You make me wanna do things I've only dreamed of.
You make me wanna fall in love!

Printed in Great Britain
by Amazon

22235500R00059